LOTUS
SUTRA
POEMS

Robley Whitson

QH
Books
1996

Lotus Sutra Poems
by
Robley Whitson

Library of Congress Catalog Card Number

95-070032

International Standard Book Number

1-55605-259-6

QH Books
Cloverdale Corporation
Bristol, IN46507-9460

Printed in the United States of America

for
Nan Adams

THE LOTUS SUTRA

The Sutra of the Lotus Flower of the Wonderful Doctrine has a unique place in the Mahayana Buddhism of China, Korea and Japan and the Vajrayana Buddhism of Tibet and Central Asia. Of the more than five thousand works that comprise the canon of Buddhist Sacred Scriptures, the Lotus Sutra is the one most widely read and certainly the one most influential in the formation of personal piety and popular religion.

The major traditions of Buddhism have a common origin in the Dharma (teaching, doctrine) of the historic Gautama twenty-five centuries ago: the Four Holy Truths—

1. the very constitution of everything is *suffering*

2. *suffering* is caused by *desire/clinging*

3. *annihilation of desire* annihilates *suffering*

4. achieved through the practice of the Noble Eight-fold Path (eight progressive realizations of the illusion of *desire-suffering*)

Although all the traditions share this original Dharma and readily recognize their mutual unity in it, they differ profoundly in their understanding of the ultimate significance of Enlightenment. For the tradition of Theravada ("the Way of the Elders") as found now in Sri Lanka and Southeast Asia, Enlightenment, Buddhahood, consists in reaching the state of Changelessness, Nirvana, in which there is an absolute annihilation of the illusory— all that *seems* to exist, including and especially the individuated human sense of being a "self," the supreme illusion to which we cling and thus the root cause of all else, the universal illusion that is *suffering.*

For the Mahayana ("Great Vehicle") tradition as found now in China, Korea and Japan, the early teaching on Nirvana as annihilation of self was but the first stage in a three-step revelatory process culminating in the Dharma of the Lotus Sutra. First the Buddha taught the Four Holy Truths as ending simply in the Changelessness of the Void. Then after this was absorbed, people were ready to receive the teaching concerning Bodhisattvas— those at the threshold of Enlightenment who out of compassion refrained from taking the final step so they could remain in the world to help in the liberation of others.

Finally, as revealed in the Lotus Sutra, the Doctrine of eternal and universal Buddhahood can at last be taught— Enlightenment is not annihilation of self: the true-self is an eternal reality embodied momentarily in time-space with its illusions of tangible reality; and the eternal true-self, one's Buddha-nature, has simply to be realized existentially by the ultimate awakening of Enlightenment.

The Dharma of the Lotus Sutra is central to Mahayana Buddhism. It is the source of the great proliferation of Buddha-identities beyond the historic Gautama— the Buddhas personifying transcendent attributes, the countless Bodhisattvas, the many mythic Buddhas that absorb pre-Buddhist traditions, and, ultimately, the myriads of true-selfs traveling the Way to the realization of their Buddhahood.

The present text of the Lotus Sutra derives from Chinese translations (made in 286 and 406 AD) of the original Sanskrit which was in written form between 50 and 150 AD. With a few exceptions (evidently later compositions) each chapter consists of a poetic section and a prose exposition of the poem. The poetic form indicates an original oral tradition much older than the written version of the first century— probably by two centuries, placing the development of this Dharma about two centuries after the death of Gautama. Further, a critical reconstruction demonstrates the poetic verses are in an early Prakritic form, while the prose is more purely Sanskritic.

With the introduction of the Lotus Sutra into China and later into Japan the text has been the source of a complex cultural development in both painting and literature. Copying the Sutra inevitably involved calligraphy, encouraging some of the most important developments in that art. Paintings and illuminations of the texts led to books of paintings of the subjects of the chapters instead of written texts. And, naturally, the chapter subjects and many of their images became integral parts of the cultural language at large.

There is a long and venerable tradition of poetry composed on the Sutra. Some poems are further reflections on the text. Others move beyond the text as such, relating the "feel" of the Sutra in poetic images to a wide range of life-meaning— indeed appropriate, considering the scope of the Lotus Dharma.

The present poems participate in the spirit of that tradition of both reflecting the Sutra and also seeking the feel of the quest to see what really is. Some poems reflect the original subject of the chapter directly, or take up an element, such as a parable. Some recast the teaching in a Western mode, such as the cycles of rebirth in terms of the space-time continuum. Some recast the scene of the chapter. And finally some take up an element as a hint to develop a new direction. In each instance a brief summary of the Sutra chapter text accompanies the poem.

Ultimately the poems seek to reverence this ancient Scripture by a celebration of its vision in the universal human quest to awaken and live in the Light. Creative words are truly creative as they beget and bring forth still newer words, that speak in strange languages, perhaps, but resonate with the power of the original. In the traditions of Wisdom there truly are universals, and these keep rising up before us— all too often to our foolish surprise. In poetry, at least, we should expect this surprise. We hope to keep finding our deepest and essential experiences made present within us through words, into images, into visions: the visions that move us from *merely* seeing to *really seeing.*

Poetry of the Sacred— seeing visions by listening to words:

> *...though not yet possessing heavenly ears,*
> *only using natural ears...*
> —Chapter XIX

I. INTRODUCTION

The Buddha, Sakyamuni, seated in meditation at Mount Grdhrakuta, the Vulture Peak, illuminates the infinite worlds and all who live in them. The attendant bodhisattvas realize he is about to teach the great and most demanding Dharma.

To the east into the sun—
into a tunnel of suns
plunging through the centers
of all the worlds,
all the worlds of worlds.

So many, many as
grains of sand
in rivers, in oceans,
sand ground to dust
blown invisible within the air
breathed unseen,
infinitesimal beginnings
of counting on, forever—
That many worlds
that many suns,
to the east.

From the Mind between two eyes
one ray of light
racing eastward
through the tunnel of suns
into their worlds
to their peoples

to the east,
always to the east,
the only direction there really is—
north, west, south

highest, lowest, center
all circle back around to it—
east where all suns arise,
so where Mind must go
to grow light alive
and wake morning mourners
from a deadly daytime.

The Mind-worlds shake
and turn to gold.
In the east-run ray
golden people see
what was never seen before:
unsleeping forests
dreaming answers
to unasked questions.

II. EXPEDIENTS

Sakyamuni proclaims that the one purpose of a Buddha is to reveal the whole truth to all. But as Buddha wisdom is so difficult to apprehend, various tactful or expedient devices must be used. Thus he reveals that previous teachings were incomplete, designed to lead to this moment. He promises ultimate Buddhahood to all, "even to children who while at play draw images of the Buddha with grass, sticks or merely with their fingernails" and so almost unwittingly take the first step on the Buddha-path.

Numbers beyond one,
counting them all:
     two, three, a few
     some, many
     then too many—
but never to all.

Just less than that,
as numerous as
brush shoots in the woods
or thin marsh reeds.
Whatever their number now
always growing into more,
too many more.
And everywhere.

Most have a wind
whirling inside them
that carries them off
in storms of twigs and leaves
blown out through a forest.

Bare earth smell
and standing trees left
to hear the light
tunneled within the sun.

The light can only reach
those who can become light—
    Those few, now light,
    who can only reach
    those who can become light—
        And those few, now light,
        and those few
            and those...

Counting them all:
    few, some, many.
But, never counting to all.

Or, ever to all:
light reaching
    few, some, many
        many and beyond
            always beyond more—
light reaching each
who can become light,
to reach another.

Numbers beyond one,
counting them all.

They never know this:
in their slightest move
they reach out,
so they stretch away.

Children playing by the sea
mounding up sand
into something not sand—
none think about it

but the mound is
something else,
a mound of Not-this.

A fingernail drawing a line,
daydream empty,
an image of something—
but an image,
a faint line of Not-that.

Just to raise a hand
or slightly bow the head
or enter a sanctuary
even by mistake—
one-step-moves
out into a light,
to be reached.

A seed within them:
    an urge
    an unease—
wherever they are
whatever they do
whoever they yet become—
met there, just that way
at that step
they take.

All the numbers counted:
none beyond one.

III. THE FIRST PARABLE: THE BURNING HOUSE

Even though there is only one path to Liberation, earlier paths thought of as complete and final were preached as preparations. In the parable of the burning house the children are unaware of their danger; their father's expedient of telling them there are wonderful playthings waiting for them entices them out and so saves their lives.

We are in this old house,
a palace of a house,
sprawling down halls
into dingy rooms
out onto porches
circled by weedy gardens.

Abandoned empty for years,
we come here to play
racing through doorways
in and out of rooms
raising a haze of dust
as we yell and laugh
daring any leftover ghost
to try to catch us.

We like this place
because it is a wreck,
already half-fallen down
so we can do anything
with no one to stop us.
And we pretend what we play,
all as real as we want
because we want it to be!

Outside someone calls to us:
    Fire! Fire!
    the whole house,
    Fire!—
Just a trick to get us
away from the fun of life
    hiding
    jumping out,
    the smash of things
    glass shatter—
all the fun of life,
patch-together ramshackle life
that falls to pieces anyway.

Now we hear someone else—
something about toys—
so we rush out to see
just as the fire runs
through the halls
into the rooms.

But,
what a liar!
No toys.

IV. THE SECOND PARABLE:
THE PRODIGAL SON

After many years of wandering, the errant son fails to recognize his father who has now become very wealthy. Step by step the father gradually draws the son back, until the day the son realizes that his powerful patron is actually his father and so comes into his rightful inheritance.

There is a Sound to be heard.
So there must be listeners
even if now they cannot hear.
It is a puzzle:
    a sound
    listeners
    not hearing—
the ever illusion of a Not-yet.

Runaways
enticed back
gently,
led step by step
as if they were
discovering
all they had lost.
But, step by step.
So, not yet.
Until they could hear
from inside
who they are—

This is my child
who left me,
wandered off—

forgot everything,
could not remember me,
or the way back.
But I searched and found
drew near
so my wonderful child
could hear me,
hear the Sound,
begin to remember
slowly, thing by thing,
finally, me.

A great mystery:
to come to hear—
to be Listener,
without the illusion of ear.

V. THE THIRD PARABLE:
THE HEALING HERBS

The Dharma is as pervasive as rain-laden clouds that enable all trees, plants and especially the healing herbs to grow. Each absorbs the same rain but in a distinctive way, just as different people follow the several Dharma-paths to the one Ultimate Truth.

The overarching world cloud
cutting across the scorch of sun,
covering a world of earth...
Grasses and trees
waiting—
all of them, so different.
Thirsts—
larger, smaller,
but always for that single cloud
full enflooding
all of them at once.

The cloud, unlike any of them—
Earth divided divided divided,
all the powdered particles,
and dry.
The growing things numberless,
and always not each other,
and dry.

A cloud of sky water
thick with pinpoint
droplets and droplets merged,
round drops interchangeably same
raining down together
slicking branches and leaves,

each a thirst
all its own.

The cloud, one only,
one with its rain,
one rich mist
flowing within itself
for those deserts
every bit of earth,
for the trees and herbs
that seem so many—
All now within that single cloud,
so unlike any of them.

VI. THE PREDICTION OF FUTURE BUDDHAHOOD

Sakyamuni foretells future Buddhahood for four disciples, who compare their joy to that of coming to a royal feast after traveling through a land of famine.

We live in a famine land,
all our lives a hunger.
Cannot imagine:
filled—
we have no word for that.
The feel of
enough—
never!
To live hungry always
is to know
that,
always,
only that.
It is a simple knowledge
excluding everything,
even ourselves—
who we might really be
if not hungry.

We would be Radiance:
a light of power
that flies in and out of eyes
dazzling them awake
to see something,
a something without a word.

We would be Moonlike:
a reflected light
softening the blind of suns,
a moon in transformations
revealed slice by slice.

We would be Lustre:
the shimmer flow
welling up from fissures
deep inside mountains,
the flicker on rivers
washed over sand,
a gold sheen
rippled over skins.

Light that becomes Fragrance:
that touches tongues,
whispering about taste
with the insistence of hunger,
that ever-present absence.

There is a feast spread for us.
But of course we hesitate.
We are too hungry.
We might not want to be
what we could come to know—

to be a Radiance
in someone's eyes

and changing

and flowing out
to someone's hunger,
to fill it with this feast
we are.

VII. THE FOURTH PARABLE: THE ILLUSORY CITY

Previous teachings about Nirvana as the ultimate goal of the Buddha-path were expedients to entice disciples to begin the journey to Enlightenment. The disciples are like travelers who become weary on an arduous journey. They stop to rest in a beautiful city which they mistake for their goal. But the city is only an illusion conjured up by their leader, and now that they are rested he can lead them to their real destination, infinitely more wonderful than the illusory city.

To be here forever,
before any of you first came
after all of you have gone—
to be the journey you make
wherever I lead you.

Everyone asks:
    How long will it take?
But long can be
a when or a where—
the time on the road
or the stretch of footsteps.
So I will tell you
the long of my forever
before and after you.

Suppose
I have such power
I can grind into powder
every possible universe

and pour it into the oceans
that flood all the worlds,
and so make an infinite ink.

Imagine
I take this ink
and travel through a thousand lands
and on the thousandth
let one drop fall.
Then travel through a thousand more
and let one more drop fall,
and so on, drop by drop
every one thousandth land.

After that I gather the lands,
the ones with the drop of ink
as well as those without,
and grind them all into powder
and then count every grain
setting each out one after another.

That is how long
my forever is—
the long of the time
to reach every thousandth land
and let fall the drop,
the long of the line
of all the grains counted out
and set in an endless row.

This is the journey you begin,
a journey of wisdom
written in lost ink drops,
a journey of light moving—
but whether fast or slow
there is nothing like it
so there is no real knowing.

I am the journey forever.
But you do not travel forever—
There will be a time and step
that bring you there then at last.

Along the way
you will grow weary
and want to turn back.
Just then I will be kind
and deceive you:
    Look! on the horizon,
    the beautiful city we seek!
You are there at last
filled with joy and ready to rest.
And so you enter the city
welcomed into its palaces
honored as victors
over all the perils of the way.

But I have deceived you.
In compassion
I evoked a mystic vision,
an unreal city
so you would rest
and not turn back.
And in compassion
I then wished it away
so you would continue on,
knowing the illusion,
so hoping in what lay ahead.

Now you are here
at the end of the journey,
the real end:
me,
everness.

VIII. THE FIFTH PARABLE: THE HIDDEN JEWEL

The disciple is like a poor man who visits a rich friend and after eating and drinking falls asleep. The generous host ties a precious jewel into the hem of his friend's shabby cloak, secretly so as not to embarrass him. After many years pass they meet again, and the rich friend, surprised at his companion's hard life, asks why he was so impoverished since he possessed a treasure all that time.

At a place and time
each of us will hear it—
The light in someone
that becomes words,
And now a light in us
becoming our words,
Then for another and another—
light to word to light,
seeing hearing.
A giving.

Friends—
a rich friend to a poor friend,
a priceless jewel given
tied into the hem of shabby clothes,
given in kindness.
Secretly,
not to embarrass
—truly friends—
and not to be thanked.
Only later discovered,
later transforming
poor into rich.

The jewel of light,
secretly a word.
There it is,
that odd lump
in our shabby clothes.
We idly finger it
so many times
until one day we look close—
    What is this thing, anyway?
We untie it.
The word of light
secretly a jewel!

We have heard it,
every one of us.
We pay no attention
but we hear it
even as we turn away.
We close our eyes
to the light always there
in someone,
someone who will not go away
will not be silent
until we become rich,
someone who will not go away.

IX. PREDICTIONS CONCERNING DISCIPLES

Disciples are rewarded with the promise of future Buddhahood.

You have heard all the words
and you remember them.
All are true:
anything ever spoken is,
but never just as spoken—
always in some other way.
You listen and listen,
then later in the dark
you jolt awake
and know the way
to hear the truth in them.

Then you choose those
which are sounds of wisdom,
from all the true words
the too few wise words.
But you must speak them all:
you cannot be the hearers—
they must listen and listen.

The world-filling wonderful sound
deep as mountains
high as oceans...
Inside that sound
a child is born,
the eldest of all,
always being born of that sound,
always eldest of all in that sound.
Parent and child always together—
whenever the sound is heard
the eldest child is seen.

And with the eldest
come all the younger
countless in their thousands.
It seems so strange—
all of them coming
just because of sounds
they once heard,
and all of them becoming
whatever the sounds said.

When they first heard
it was endless words,
telling them so many things
and they said:
    Yes! and
    Yes! and
    Yes!

But breath by breath words dropped,
fewer and fewer to be heard.
So they had to listen and listen.
They said:
    Yes!

X. Teachers of the Dharma

The promise of Buddhahood is made to anyone who honors the teaching of the Lotus Sutra in any way: who receives, keeps, reads, recites, explains or copies it; who venerates it; who teaches even one phrase to one person; who enshrines the text. To preach the Sutra one must have compassion for all, forbearance, and realize the phenomenal emptiness of Truth, its No-Thingness.

Ice over winter ocean water,
sunned air raising a mist above—
swim the water,
walk the ice,
fly the mist.

The floor of desert dust—
if there is water
it is deep below,
and the high haze in the sky
is too thin for clouds.

The two waters:
the everywhere-water,
the perhaps-somewhere-water.

Digging down through sand
to find somewhere-water—
as long as grains are dry
they are the hope,
hope that breathes away
with the first moist hint,
then vanishes in wet hands.

To return from nowhere
vowing now never to leave—
to begin to wake them.

The first drop of a single word:
something compassionate, said or done,
someone gently saying, doing.

Thousands there to see it,
or, no one at all.

XI. The Vision of the Jeweled Shrine

A wondrous jeweled shrine rises into midair from within the earth. Innumerable buddhas with their attendant bodhisattvas gather from all the worlds. The shrine is opened, revealing the Eternal Buddha enthroned. Sakyamuni Buddha enters and sits beside him, and then preaches on the difficulty in teaching the Dharma.

We are so easily amazed—
a dazzling sanctuary
raised to the sky,
all our awe tight upon
the blaze of facets
and a glow of gold.

Always surfaces,
all we sense is surface:
our own skins shiver
mirroring the flash.

There is a voice
from deep within the shrine,
so we stop looking.
We must listen.

Listening happens inside—
hearing words from someone,
but the words enter,
move in our minds
speak to other words,
our own words.

Behind the door of the shrine
is someone who comes
from the world of truth,
a world the Void of Thing.
But the door is only surface,
part of gold and glitter,
our closed skins.

As we listen inside
to that inside-voice
our rush of words moves
into every shape there could be.

So we begin to see
—awe-free—
two enthroned together:
the mutable Eternal,
the absolute Momentary.

XII. DEVADATTA / THE PRINCESS

The first story is that of the king who renounced all to seek Enlightenment, and offered himself as the servant of Devadatta, a seer who subsequently became an enemy of the Way. By his humility in serving such a one, the king came to Buddhahood. Next, to the great surprise of all the disciples, the Buddha reveals that Buddhahood is open to women, given in the story of the eight year old daughter of the king of the seas. She offered the Buddha the gift of a priceless pearl as an act of reverence and was thereupon transformed into a buddha.

She brings a pearl,
the irritant grit of sand
healed into a round tear,
moon luminous
within a clot of slime
within a layered shell
within a muddy ooze
within the sea.

She gives him the pearl,
from her hand into his.
He takes the pearl,
into his hand from hers.
In that instant-moment
the pearl changes:
hers,
now
his.
    He feels
the smooth round
    she remembers.

Out of the dark
into the light—
just that fast.
The first ray strikes.
That instant—
    Before: dark
    Now: light.

Or that moment is
lifetime in infinity
each an infinitesimal change,
    steps
            missteps
                    stumble steps
through dark wanderings.
All the groping and grasping;
never content—
always a next and a next
    hoping.

One of the countless steps
is the right one
—know it or not—
then all the rest
take us to the last.

From the beginning lightless
but somehow knowing
—a desperate guess—
an Other than the dark.
The irritant grit within
that never lets us stop,
even scratching
the eyes of our dreams
blurring them with tears.
Tears one day
finally
lenses for the light,
prisms splaying it into color.

XIII. FORTITUDE

*The disciples promise to expound
the Sutra, in all the worlds and in
this wicked world as well, whatever
the perils, even if they must lay
down their lives for it.*

A vow over words—
to speak them, ponder them
to float them black
on scrolls of white paper,
a flow in winter water
between ice banks.

To vow life
for the sounds of these words,
for the sound these words create
as they reach someone else.
A vow to create,
reaching all or some or one—
perhaps reaching no one.
Even so, a creation
now about to happen,
a whole new world.

On an unmoving earth,
one side always day
the other ever night
with a ring of twilight between,
a hunter and lion roam.
They search the two horizons,
the always day, the ever night,
first one then the other.
So they never meet,
though the twitching lion tail
almost flicks the hunter's back.

They know each is there
somewhere in the half-light
but they must make no sound.

At a sound
they would have to turn,
see each other,
surprised.
They would have to create
something together:
a killing,
vowing away life.
In that old unmoving earth
there is a vow over words:
never speak them—
create nothing.

XIV. THE SIXTH PARABLE:
THE CROWN JEWEL

In teaching the Dharma the disciples must conduct themselves prudently, and stress peaceful practices leading people to the Truth by subtle methods, a compassionate manner and simple parables. In the parable of the crown jewel a wise king rewards his soldiers for their valor and loyalty with great riches. He keeps his crown jewel, however, since only a king may wear it. But at the final victory he gives that too, for the victors have become themselves kingly. And so the Buddha now gives this crowning jewel, the Lotus Sutra.

Body
among bodies
moving here amidst others,
together forming a here,
ever-changing here.
Outside,
moving to others—
deeds reaching out to them.
Inside,
always the same—
a forest solitude.

Mouth
lips shaping words
sounds being heard
that mean other words—
when spoken forever,
sounds of every other word.
All from two lips,
all from one mouth,

so every word
gentle, kind—
words that can be heard.

Mind
seeing, recognizing
turned to faces, not thoughts.
A mind filled with people:
the deeply venerated,
all those alive in light
for those who still sleep,
the ignored, the despised
who cannot see themselves
in the blind dark—
who are seen so clearly
in a mind of light.

Vow
to be that light until
the very last awakens.

A triumphant host,
and the rewards of their king—
lands and treasures,
all the king has except
the jewel in the crown.
But he gives this too.
They are amazed:
this jewel is only for kings.
Indeed, it is!
for kings who
by their bodily deeds
their kindly spoken words
their enlightening minds
awaken every last one.

If you should dream
what will you see?
Golden bodies radiating light.
Thrones for roaring lions.
The Void as it is:
unmoving not receding or turning,
just like Space.

You will see the Lamp extinct
beyond the last of the flame
when the smoke ends.

XV. Welling Up Out of the Earth

There are innumerable bodhisattvas in this world already converted by Sakyamuni— yet the disciples find this hard to believe, since he has just begun his mission in a world aeons old. They tell him it is as difficult to believe as it is for a young man to point to an old man and call him son rather than father.

Someone must come
from beyond the space of our world,
drop out of the sky
just before the moment
we are to perish.
There must be worlds
filled with benevolent saviors.
There are,
but they do not come.

We have our own,
who spring up everywhere
from this life-rich earth
like shoots of careless seeds
wherever a patch of soil
or rock crack of dirt
lets in a root.
Some are lion-eager thunderers,
others quiet-to-invisible—
all of them consumed
with us, every one of us,
with me.

So our world space
and flying sky
are empty for us

to rise and fill them
with all new stars
set on fire by...
actually, by nothing—
by seeing through the illusion
of spaces and skies:
as if already crowded
with stars and clouds
with no room for us,
as if teeming with saviors
about to pluck us
from our world,
the world we know—
ours,
not theirs.

They look on
at this puzzle we are:
children begetting their own parents;
young smooth faces
bearing
agèd wrinkled faces;
sons and daughters old,
mothers and fathers young.

Our puzzle is saying something
about the perish moment—
something about
moment:
the When of it, of us.
Perhaps When is
just as easily
backward as forward—
like those illusions
of spaces and skies,
some sort of moment
unlocated.

XVI. THE SEVENTH PARABLE: THE WISE PHYSICIAN

Sakyamuni Buddha reveals he is eternal, infinite in time and space. In the parable, children of a physician though gravely ill refuse to take the bitter tasting medicine he prescribes. They then hear a falsified report that their father has died. Out of remorse at having rejected his help they now take the medicine and are cured. The father returns and they realize his love in deceiving them to save them from their foolishness.

We come upon a burning light,
burning long before we came,
and however long we gaze
the light keeps burning.
If we were to go
it still would burn.

Ever drawn to light
we fail to see the burning,
something consumed, drawn in—
the burning
before we came
after we go:
that light, now.
Before and after
light,
now that we are here,
burning.

Still we fail to see.
Oh, we look, stare hard.
Not enough!
In front of our eyes,

inside them,
it is always the light.
We can never really see
that burning
going on now and before and after.
If only we could separate
the light from the burning...

The burning— consuming, perishing.
Delirium.
There is one desperate cure:
to shock the dying awake
the physician
must seem to die.

The light, that shape
bright in our eyes
seemingly simply there
is not there at all,
never was, never could be—
the illusion of a forever
in a blinding.

Forever is merely long,
an immensity of time,
of things changing—
An unimagined amount:
the long of all that burning.

If we could just separate
light from
burning from
burning light
to see in between them—

Only there,
no coming or going,
no unreal
no more-real.

XVII. DISCRIMINATION OF MERITS

The Buddha asserts that those who read, disseminate or expound the Sutra will behold Sakyamuni, and see the common dirt of the earth is actually precious lapis lazuli.

In the shift of shadows
mountains become other things:
the dreamed shapes of sound,
sound much simpler than words.
So from everywhere we come
to hear the mountain dream
and learn the less-than-word
in the darks of its rocks.

To speak one almost-word,
that can never be a meaning,
is to become one of the things
mountains can become:
to be the one seekers come to
to hear the mountain dream
the shape of that word.

The shadows of the summit
are the dream of a vulture—
the spread of black wings
in search of the dead,
neck and head-skin featherless
for the reach within rot,
the dread bird of life
dropping from the sky
with its meaningless word—

able to make that sound,
to know what that word
never means,

to see the strike of light,
the shadow cast,
but no rock—
then to say it:

Mountains Eternally Dreams
Dreams Eternally Mountains—

My Eternal Body,
always in Illusion—

But, always!

Any who see me
are the Shape.
Any who speak
are Dream.

XVIII. THE MERITS OF JOYFUL ACCEPTANCE

The Buddha asserts that if one expounds the Sutra to a second, the second to a third, and so on, the fiftieth (or whoever) hearing it will be as joyous as the first and receive as many benefits.

Humid summer nights—

Fireflies everywhere
silently starring the dark,
eye-blink dots of light
flying invisible patterns.

The bubble clusters
clinging to reed stems
in warm marsh water,
a foam of eggs
about to happen.

A heavy blend of smells
the breath of plants
our own breath—
irresistible-pull inside.

These and every other universe,
all our urgent worlds
offering us mere moments—
flicker of light,
another bit of life,
a pause.

A whirled mix of things
pleasures, pains, the inbetweens—
easily touched,
not possessed.
The wind of moments.

We live
always moving on
always trying not to,
something in us somehow
saying: stay!
We would, if we could.
Or, is that mirror-backward?—
We could, if we would.

In one of those breath pauses:
to wait
not move to the next,
feel the wind around us
for what it is—
only a rush away.

So we stay and wait,
sit here, listening,
test what we hear
by the only measure:
Joy!
not pleasure,
Joy!
not the infinities of pleasure
always infinitely lost
with the things whirled off,
Joy!
hearing even one word of
who I am,
Joy! inviting another to sit
here beside me,
hear with me
who we are.

XIX. The Merits of a Preacher

The Buddha asserts that anyone who reads, recites, interprets or disseminates the Sutra will attain innumerable merits. By hearing only a single phrase anyone will realize unlimited meanings and perceive the reality of everything.

We are not yet born
already we have shaped ourselves
into powers to
see and hear
smell and taste
feel and know—
all of these to feed upon
the world we will enter,
but only later.

In the months of our beginning
our powers feed upon ourselves
dreaming dreams of ourselves
hearing our own songs,
growing into ourselves from within
not bounded by objects.
So, we must already be,
always, before things happen.

We are born, and forget—
almost completely,
until something does happen,
a different something for each of us—
say, the fragrance of someone,
a taste that feeds us.
Then it is
beginning again
and power again.

We reach out into lives,
so many are there for us.
We become aware of them
but can no longer grasp
who is outside
who is inside—
or how to choose words
that can even say this,
the feel we do not know.

But we begin to speak anyway,
the first words that come,
phrases, bits of sentences
images, feelings.
Amazing! they all take our shape.
Everything we say says: us!
And as we say more and more
it becomes the whole-us.

If I proclaim just one sentence
my body is suddenly crystal,
clear nearly invisible—

Anyone can see through
one side to the other,
and all the surfaces
sparkling mirror faceted
catch the gazing of everyone—

All of us inside
all of us outside
embracing unbounded,
already always.

XX. The Bodhisattva Named Never-Despising

Sakyamuni reveals that he was formerly a bodhisattva who was always kind to all and venerated all regardless of how much he was insulted or threatened with harm. Thus those who preach this Sutra must be ever steadfast in compassion.

Scorn—
listen to that sound!
If the word were unknown
we would still hear
Harsh.
There is a mean feel to it
and to that whole clutch
of harsh words:
despise, contemn, disdain—
Mean to someone.

Scorning no one,
reverencing.
Revere—
a rising sound,
rising to meet someone
who draws others up,
not one exalted above others.

A gentle sage comes
revering all of us.
What a fool!
He cannot see us
scrambling over others,
frantically jumping up and down
like selfish children
desperate to be singled out.

He cannot be aware of us
so smugly More—
there is always someone less.

We do not want to be revered,
not all of us—
not all of us the same,
not all of us rising.
There must be some
left behind.

But that fool says: No!
All of us are the light
filled with its power.
Creators.
Transformers.
That is all he ever does:
revere us.
He knows no sacred words,
is never wrapped in awe.
He simply reveres us.

Empty wisdom.
Emptiest!

XXI. Transcendent Powers of the Buddha

As is true of all buddhas gathered together, the Buddha voice and radiance reach even the farthest worlds. The mere sound of clearing their throats or snapping their fingers reverberates throughout all worlds louder than thunder.

We stand invisible in the sky,
as invisible as is the sky,
so the wonder of it
remains hidden.
When we speak
the words from our tongues
reach everywhere at once,
so none can hear
the separate sounds.
We radiate light
every color filling the universe
with too much beauty,
so they grow tired
and sleep.

It is all there
in overwhelming power,
nothing held back
nothing yet to come.
But they listen only
to the humming of dreams,
watch only the light-flickerings
behind their closed eyes.

Awaiting their waking
we are here, the two of us,
the Momentary, the Eternal,
the infinity of us
here, anywhere:

in an awe-filled temple
in an oracular grove
at the roots of a tree
within a colonnaded solitude
in a simple house
in a sumptuous palace
on a mountain summit
at the floor of a valley
beyond a wilderness—
Everyplace sanctuaries,
all of them
Thrones of Enlightenment
readied for their rising.

XXII. ENTRUSTING THE DHARMA

Sakyamuni rises from his throne, places his hands three times on the heads of the countless bodhisattvas and entrusts the teaching of the Dharma to them.

Hand of blessing
on all our heads.
I feel the touch—
hardly any weight
to those fingertips
yet a sweep of power—
not an overwhelming
but a welling up
from unguessed depth.

An ocean bottom chasm
where the rock crust splits
in a molten gush
of fire and water together,
and I can grow into everywhere
if I wish it.
And I say: Yes!
We all say: Yes!

The power of that hand
is placed into all our hands
to be hands of blessing,
gentle hands always extended
to give— to give what?
Hands always empty
because emptied
in the giving,
the endless giving away.

In that ocean chasm,
the heart fire poured out,

earth giving itself away
into the cold deep of water,
and so the earth rising
slowly rising to the surface—
the rock of new lands,
islands of seeds.

So now all who came to us,
drawing us up from shadow
into the invisible sky,
themselves vanish
in their own emptied hands
infinitely gone into blessing.
We are left
each one alone
I am left—
Hands filled with the power
to become emptied hands.

XXIII. THE BODHISATTVA NAMED MEDICINE-KING

Medicine-King Bodhisattva was so grateful for receiving the gift of the Dharma that he sacrificed his own body as a burnt offering. This bears witness to the limitless power and benefits of the Sutra, valued more than bodily life. Anyone, women as well as men, hearing the Sutra recited will find Enlightenment in the Paradise of Amitabha Buddha.

Storms of illusions sweep
a world so easily fooled—
thinking the sun burns
or the moon does not,
thinking trees are alive
and animals
and even people.

The delusions of dreaming:
during all the long nights
the daylight seems so real,
and we do things
we cannot do—
until we wake surprised
in a different kind of day,
confused remembering.

Everything is always ending
but never complete,
always slipping away or fading,
desire feeding desire
for something, something.

The illusions hurt,
sharp rough edges cut
away at whatever we are
yet never reach us.
So they never finish us
and we linger on.
The cure is fire—
not the fire that destroys
into smoke and ash—
that fire already rages
in the tangle of illusions
burning and smothering us.

The cure is our own fire,
consuming not destroying,
turning us into light
so we can see inside
deep under the surfaces
to what is really there,
to see past the dreams
of all those somethings
we stretch for with hands
we no longer have,
or have to have.

What we really see
is simply so beautiful.

That is what we want—
who we want.

XXIV. THE BODHISATTVA NAMED WONDERFUL-SOUND

Wonderful-Sound Bodhisattva comes from another world to see Sakyamuni, who explains that Wonderful-Sound appears in many different forms in order to expound the Sutra to different hearers.

The voice shimmers with gold.
Wherever it is heard
golden people appear—
they might be new people,
or just people who listen
and become gold with the words.

The voice they hear stammers,
words and bits of words
stumbling together in spurts.
Many are baffled
and drift off to other sounds.
Others listen closely
and puzzle with the patterns.

The stuttered pieces
are the shattered elements
for making inside worlds,
as many worlds as hearers—
So there must be infinitely
more elements and kinds
than those shaped into a world
small enough to be there
outside the ears
of the golden hearers.

Inside Mind-worlds
can never stay inside—
They flash out,

unlike the small world
growing itself from its center,
sphering into the empty blank—
however fast it grows,
at every moment
it is this sphere only,
and not yet more.

Mind-worlds are simply there,
complete
infinitely encompassing,
there at the moment of thought
the instant a word is heard,
any stammered bit of word.
Mind-worlds, suddenly there,
embrace the small world
and all the possible worlds
in that flash of hearing.

The glorious stuttering voice
scatters into every ear
and everyone creates a world
that is all worlds—
all caught in the pauses,
infinitesimal pauses,
between the sputtered sounds
that shimmer of gold.

XXV. The Universal Gate of Avalokitesvara

The Bodhisattva named Attentive-to-the-Cries-of-the-World will free from harm those who cry out, as he appears in countless diverse forms according to the situation of need.

We live in a vast temple—
its courts stretch over lands
walled apart by mountains;
its fountains and pools
rivers and flooding seas;
sun and moon, stars and dust
its countless lights arched above.

A sanctuary never silent:
cries, deafening cries—
any mystic songs or mantic chants
shouted down by ceaseless cries.
Pain, need, dread,
even the dull drain-away—
we cry out.

The sounds say something else:
there is someone to hear.

If only everyone would
stop, keep quiet
my cry could be heard!
I hope someone listens,
can hear me.
If only there were silence
or if I could cry out louder.

Someone must be there,
otherwise why would we know
to cry out at hurt

—instantly, impulsion—
know someone can help.
Every cry is the word:
Come, Oh please come!

It is hard enough
to hope for myself—
but everyone crying out
all at once all calling:
Here, over here, me, me!

Too many voices, too many.

But if there is someone—
if that is why we cry out
unthinkingly,
our mouths and throats
always ready with that word—
perhaps all of us are heard,
perhaps one who heeds me
can heed all of us...

It could be so simple—
each cries out,
each hears.

XXVI. THE ALL-PRESERVING FORMULARIES

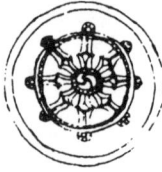

Various bodhisattvas vow to protect those devoted to the Sutra and its Dharma, each employing a dharani (mystical formulary in Sanskrit, derived from divine names) for this purpose.

Ancient rituals of words
repeated rhythm jumble syllables,
mythic names
half-names
bits of names—
everything almost remembered.

The ritual words mean nothing.
Once perhaps— not now.
They have worn thin,
chanted too often.
But there is something left
in those who mouth them.
They reach out
with old empty sounds,
but they do reach out
to hold all of us
from leaching away
into arid illusion.

Incantation breathed in awakening—

Inexhaustible
Incomprehensible
Illimitable—
swarming, teeming
more always more
almost too much more.

Incantation flickered in lights—

Fire, flames of fire
Fireballs ablaze
Flashed sparks—
fevered, seething
burned and burned
unconsumed.

Incantation fleshed in bodies—

Corrode: No!
Ravage: No!
Decay: No!—
nothing rusted to less
not withered old, gone
none wasted.

Incantation voiced in myriads—

Sounds
countless crowds
Resound
Loud
drowning shouts
now in every mouth
echo infinite echo.

Not even dreams
can silence
invisible breaths
unbinding spells.

XXVII. THE KING NAMED RESPLENDENCE

A king had two sons who wished to go to hear the teaching of the Buddha. After demonstrating miraculous powers they persuaded their father to permit it. The king and his queen went with them and all four were converted to the Dharma. The king is amazed to be able to encounter a buddha, an event as rare as the encounter of the one-eyed tortoise with the eye-sized hole in the log (an image from the Samyuttanikaya scripture).

The ancient one-eyed tortoise—
oldest tortoise ever was,
old as the ocean it swims,
old as the first foam,
the original wave,
the tide that swelled
when the moon was born.

The tortoise swims the seas
deep underneath
on and on everywhere
wherever the water covers,
countless ages forever.

Back at the beginning
of the one-eyed tortoise
and the earliest sea,
the ancient tree that bore
the seeds of all the trees,
storm-stripped of bark
of every branch and twig,
fell into that sea:

a great trunk of wood
pierced through with a hole,
a single hole
just the size of a tortoise eye.

The beam floats the seas
rolling the surface
on and on everywhere
wherever the water covers,
countless ages forever.

Once each hundredth year
the tortoise paddles up
from the deep it swims
to look at the sky
in a moment of light,
then plunges down again
to swim through the dark
another hundred years.

Oh how long it will be,
the countless centuries,
before the wallowing log
floats to the one chance spot
where the half-blind tortoise
will raise its head
and finally peer at the sky
through that single hole
the size of a tortoise eye!

That long, that rare
to meet oneself in light—
Or, instantly awake
at the beginning.

XXVIII. THE ENCOURAGEMENT OF THE BODHISATTVA NAMED UNIVERSAL-VIRTUE

Universal-Virtue Bodhisattva asks Sakyamuni how one is to realize the Dharma of the Lotus Sutra after the Buddha enters phenomenal extinction. He is told: one must be in the protective thoughts of all the Buddhas, must practice all the virtues, have right concentration and the desire to rescue all beings. Universal-Virtue vows to commit himself to this path; the image of the wondrous elephant.

I come to wake sleepers
who dream without remembering,
who know they have forgotten.
They can almost touch it—
they reach out,
it slips by.
They almost speak the word
that will begin it—
the first sound
will not shape itself.

Their dreams are too full,
every thing there might be
all tumbled together—
so I come to them
in one overpowering form
atop a six-tusked elephant.

From its trunk a flower grows,
a golden bud about to bloom.
As it opens a ray flashes
from the trunk to the eyes
from the eyes to the ears.

Then illuminating the head
it becomes a golden cup
overflowing with light.

My elephant strides the world
on seven pylon legs.
In the print of each foot
a thousand more elephants rise up,
with every seven steps
seven thousand elephants.

We appear in majestic procession
moving through the world
now thousands
now millions
incalculably ever more.

I sit enthroned upon its back
radiating myriad color lights
through the eyes and ears
into the dreaming minds
of all the sleepers
as elephant universes
trample down the jumble
of everything forgotten.

And you begin to remember
how to speak the word
that begins awakening.